TH

Supernatural

Effect

Confessions of How One Small Show

Had Such a Huge Impact

KELLIE VUICHARD

NEWMAN SPRINGS PUBLISHING
320 Broad Street
Red Bank, NJ 07701

First originally published by Newman Springs Publishing 2021
Cover design by Kristy Napoli

ISBN 978-1-63881-589-1 (Paperback)
ISBN 978-1-63881-590-7 (Digital)

Printed in the United States of America

To Punkin and Noodles, my Sam and Dean

Love, Mom

INTRODUCTION

What do two brothers, a 1967 Chevy Impala nicknamed Baby, classic rock music, demons, monsters, an awkward fallen angel in a trench coat, a salvage yard, a bunker, God, and the Kansas song "Carry On Wayward Son" all have in common? To most people, absolutely nothing at all—but to millions of fans worldwide, it can only mean one thing: *Supernatural*, the show that just recently ended its fifteen-year, 327-episode run on the CW and has spawned books, an anime series, merchandise, conventions, and several successful charities, along with several different Facebook, Instagram, and Twitter followers and fan groups.

Anyone who is a fan of the show knows that it is much more than a sci-fi/horror show about the things that go bump in the night. It is about the love and loyalty of two brothers, how family doesn't end in blood, how you always have free will and no one's story is written.

The Road Begins

The TV show was created by Eric Kripke and starred Jensen Ackles (Dean Winchester) and Jared Padalecki (Sam Winchester).

It was first broadcast on September 13, 2005, on what was The WB and subsequently became part of The CW's lineup; it is the only show to appear under both network names. The show has gone into syndication, playing on streaming services such as Netflix and cable stations such as TNT. However, the show almost never was. The show was in development for several years as creator Eric Kripke spent that time unsuccessfully pitching it. Finally, after ten years of pitching his idea, The WB television network finally decided to pick it up and run with it, causing one of the biggest fandoms to ever be spawned, ranking it up there with the *Star Trek* and *Doctor Who* fandoms.

The pilot episode was first broadcast on September 13, 2005, and was viewed by an estimated 5.69 million viewers, and ratings of the first four episodes quickly prompted the WB to pick it up for a full season. The show under Kripke was only intended for a three-season run, but that was later extended to five. At the conclusion of the fifth season, the show's main storyline ended as Kripke departed the series as showrunner, handing the reins over to various showrunners such as Sera Gamble, Jeremy Carver, Robert Singer, and Andrew Dabb. In the eleventh season, *Supernatural* became the longest-running American live-action fantasy TV series. On November 19, 2020, we said goodbye to *Supernatural* as the series concluded, ending its fifteen-year run.

The Big Question

So what's the appeal of the show? That's what I wanted to know; I'm not a fancy doctor or professional with an impressive PhD behind my name. I am just a mom, a wife, a writer, and a fan myself. So I took to the fan pages and started conducting interviews and started doing my own research and found out some interesting facts. I wanted to know what makes this fandom so different from any other out there. I mean we have all seen them or at least we think we have an idea of what they look like anyway. The Trekkies, the Whovians, the ones who cosplay as their favorite characters from movies, shows, or comic books. So what makes the *Supernatural* fandom any different from any of its counterparts?

First of all, the fans follow a simple creed upheld by the show itself, "Family doesn't end in blood." So the fans and the fandom in a sense are one great big family—all races, all creeds, all genders, no one is excluded. It's a safe space for one and all. Second is the actors themselves; they have made themselves visible and accessible to the fans from the start, and they have also acknowledged themselves as part of the family and recognized the deep connection with their fans and that, without their support, the show wouldn't have been as successful as it was.

All of the actors had prior acting careers before *Supernatural*. Ackles appeared on *Days of Our Lives*, Padalecki was on *Gilmore Girls*. While much of the story lines are surrounded around Dean and Sam Winchester, it's the ensemble cast that brings it all together and brings the feeling of family through, whether the character is good, bad, or indifferent. Not only are the characters scared and flawed, so are the actors who play them, and they know that and have opened up countless times about fighting their own demons, whether it has been addiction, depression, homelessness, lack of self-worth, or any number of personal wounds; they have been extremely candid about their battles and winning them. And the fans have openly embraced and shown their love and support for them.

The Angel, the Nerd, and the Bad Boy

Misha Collins, born Dmitri Tippens Krushnic, was cast as Castiel, the angel who made his first appearance in season 4 episode 1, "Lazarus Rising," where his entrance as the raspy-voiced angel is still talked about in the fan groups. To quote some fans, "He walked in like a boss." The character was originally supposed to only appear in four episodes but went on to become as much of a fan favorite as Sam and Dean and made his final appearance in season 15 episode 18, "Despair."

Collins was born in Boston and had a hard life starting out. His family was poor and oftentimes homeless, and yet he has taken those struggles and turned them around for a source of inspiration and good works. One might say Collins is a jack-of-all-trades"; he worked as a carpenter and woodworker in New England's Berkshire Mountains. He graduated from the University of Chicago with honors and a BA in social theory. He was an intern for four months at the White House during the Clinton administration in the office of presidential personnel and also worked at the National Public Radio headquarters in Washington, DC.

Collins is a published poet, with his writings being in such literary journals as the *Columbia Poetry Review* and the *California Quarterly*. Collins, along with his wife Vicki, also coauthored a cookbook titled *The Adventurous Eaters Club*. The cookbook focuses on family time mixed with healthy eating with kid-friendly recipes designed for kids of all ages to have fun with and make messes in the kitchen, along with helpful hints and tricks thrown in to help start little ones out on the right path to healthy eating. According to reports, most of the book's sales have gone to charitable organizations specializing in food nutrition. He is also the founder of two charities, Random Acts and GISH. Random Acts promotes random acts of kindness and also helps to build orphanages, schools, provide clean water, and mobilize people all over the world.

GISH stands for Greatest International Scavenger Hunt and is an eight-time Guinness World Record-setting experience that brings out the weird, creative, and adventurous side of people all while doing good. GISH is in over a hundred countries as well and, trust me, I speak from firsthand experience when I say it is a total blast and a life changer.

Entry fees from participants, otherwise known as GISHers, go to charities across the country and around the world. Teams are composed of fifteen players with a list of items or tasks to be completed that is issued at the start of the hunt. An item can be anything—from doing a random act of kindness to creating a Skittles portrait to making a wearable outfit from recyclable wrapping paper. The items are selected to promote out-of-the-box thinking with creativity, social awareness, and art, all while doing good works and having fun and connecting with others in a weird, wacky environment. GISH has raised money for everything from feeding over 1 million children during COVID shutdowns to going in and removing landmines in Laos, to providing fresh water, planting trees, and raising awareness on social justice issues. They hold one main hunt in the summer and several smaller hunts throughout the year. I was lucky enough to participate in the Halloween Hunt in 2020, even with COVID in full effect; it was a great way to connect with people and have fun. The GISH community is much more than just the hunts; however, they have their own Facebook page and many small offshoots of that for pen pals, writers, getting in shape, and an overall support group of people. GISH actually restored my faith in humanity.

When I joined, the world had me so beaten down, and I have met so many people in the different groups that I know I will probably never meet face to face, but when facing an issue that I may be nervous about, they are always there with a kind word. GISH recently held a six-hour micro hunt called GISH Fest on May 22, 2021. It was a way to celebrate the end of what seemed like never-ending isolation for many. There was a six-hour Zoom, dancing, interacting with fellow GISHers, and most importantly, weird, wacky fun event for a good cause. One of the items on the hunt list was a fundraiser for India, which unfortunately is still in the grips of COVID-19. The goal was $25 to help provide oxygen concentrators, PPEs, and other supplies to the people of India. GISHers not only met but beat and broke the barrier by raising over $75,000, helping over 1,500 families and their communities. The capacity of the people involved to love and give is overwhelming.

On September 7, 2018, Misha Collins purchased a star for the *Supernatural* family. He was quoted as saying, "Whenever you look up at the night sky, you'll know you are not alone." That statement became something much bigger, and the fan support was overwhelming. Misha, along with Jensen Ackles, started the #SPNFamily Crisis Network in partnership with Random Acts, TWLOHA, and IMAlive. The online support network helps fans cope with mental health issues such as depression, self-injury, and addiction; in addition, it also provides training to fan volunteers who wish to be crisis responders in their spare time. The network also provides immediate access to support lifelines for anyone in crisis and local community resources for those needing additional support or information. The project was launched on February 12, 2016, with a T-shirt fundraiser and 1,500 fans signed up to be volunteers. By March 4, Misha had tweeted that 8,500 fans had volunteered to staff the crisis network. And if all that wasn't enough to keep the man busy, he has several other TV show guest spots, movies, directing, and producer roles to his name. Among them *Moving Alan*, a movie where he starred alongside future *Supernatural* star Mark Pelligrino (2003), *Stonehenge Apocalypse* (2011), and *Divine: The Series* (2011).

> If you can make a difference for
> one person, then it's worth it.
> —Jared Padalecki

A native of Texas, Jared Padalecki (Sam Winchester) and wife, Genevive (Ruby), also a cast member, traveled to the state capitol in 2017 to help advocate for David's Law, a Texas law that targets cyberbullying, named for David Molak, a sixteen-year-old Alamo Heights High School student who committed suicide in January of 2016. The San Antonio police said accusations of online bullying by other students of Molak surrounded his death. Padalecki was quoted as saying, "I wasn't always six four" and an actor. If a child gets suspended for punching somebody, decides instead to bombard that same person with endless messages of "You're worthless, you should hurry up and kill yourself" or "This school and this world would be better off without you," and we simply kowtow to the rules, we stand idly by and comfort ourselves with the excuse that our hands were tied, "It wasn't on school grounds," "It's beyond our control." That is true cowardice.

David's Law makes cyberbullying that leads to the injury or suicide of a minor a misdemeanor. It also requires public schools to report the bullying and intervene.

Always Keep Fighting (AKF) is a campaign started by Jared through Represent.com in March 2015. The first campaign raised money for To Write Love on Her Arms, which supports people struggling with different mental health issues. The cause is extremely close to Jared's heart as he has been very open and candid about his own struggles and battles with depression. Jared, in his passion to bring awareness and remove the stigma surrounding these issues, has been quoted as saying, "If someone has cancer, they're not embarrassed to have cancer. They know it's not their fault. But if someone is depressed, they assume that people are going to look at them like they have three heads. Hopefully, this is helping to start a conversation."

During a convention in Minneapolis, a fan stood up during the Q&A portion of the panel and began having a minor panic attack. As she stood struggling to get the words out, Ackles and Padalecki's responses went from that of joking around to genuine concern. The fan wanted to tell the duo how much the Always Keep Fighting campaign has meant to her but instead was only able to say, "On behalf of the fandom, thank you for starting such a great campaign." Jared Padalecki thanked her for her support, and both he and Jensen Ackles ran to the end of the stage and laid down to hug her.

Before *Supernatural*, Padalecki starred on *Gilmore Girls* as Dean Forester. By bringing pop-cultural references into the episodes, the writers of *Supernatural*, who were known for their use of breaking the fourth wall and using meta in the show several times, used both Padalecki's and Ackles's past acting careers to their advantage. With Jared in the episode titled "Hollywood Babylon" (S2 E18), Sam and Dean are on a movie set taking a tour as the tour guide makes a remark about the *Gilmore Girls* set. Sam starts to look uncomfortable and turns to his brother who gives him a big smile and a thumbs-up. Sam exits the tram.

Padalecki started appearing in TV shows such as *ER* in 1999 and *Young MacGyver*. He has an uncredited part in *Cheaper by the Dozen* as the bully and also appeared in *House of Wax* and *Friday the13th*. He is now not only the lead actor in the new CW series *Walker*, but he is also the producer of the show as well. In 2020, he starred in *I Choose Life: Stories of Suicide and Survival*. It is an independent film documentary by Jacqui Blue and with the help of others such as T.O.N.E-z, Kevin Briggs and Montes, and Ciera Danielle. The in-depth film covers not only the five-thousand-year history through today where suicide is at crisis levels and the second leading cause of death in our nation's youth, but it also has a very clear and concise discussion about the topic.

Jensen Ackles (Dean Winchester), also a Texas native, is an actor, singer, producer, and director. Unlike Collins or Padalecki, Jensen had an on-and-off modeling career since the age of four. In

1996, at the age of eighteen, he began to concentrate on his acting career and had several guest roles on different TV shows such as *Mr. Rhodes* and *Sweet Valley High* before joining the cast of NBC's *Days of Our Lives*, which again the writers of *Supernatural* used to their advantage in the episode "French Mistake," where the boys are Sam and Dean playing Jensen and Jared playing Sam and Dean. Did you get that? Dean walks into Jensen's trailer and sees an episode of *Days of Our Lives* with him in it and is less than happy about it. In 1998, he won the Soap Opera Digest Award for Best Male Newcomer and was nominated three times for a Daytime Emmy for Outstanding Younger Actor in a Drama series. He, too, has had guest spots and recurring roles in several TV shows such as *Dark Angel*, *Dawson's Creek*, and *Smallville*. He took the lead in the cult remake of *My Bloody Valentine 3D* and was given high praise for his comedic timing in the independent film *Ten Inch Hero*, in which he costarred with his future wife, Danneel Harris. He has also provided the voice for Jason Todd in *Batman: Under the Red Hood* and for the caped crusader himself in *Batman: The Long Halloween*. Besides this, he has done voice work for Disney Interactive Studios. He was the voice of a character named Gibson in the video game Tron: Evolution. Ackles had sung for years alongside other cast members such as Rob Benedict and Richard Speight Jr. as an extra treat for the fans. He finally released his first single as a professional singer titled "The Sounds of Someday" in 2019. Ackles, along with musician Steve Carlson, collaborated to form Radio Company and the debut album was called *Radio Company Vol. 1*. Their second album *Radio Company Vol. 2* was released May 2020 and went to number 1 on Spotify.

Ackles recently joined the cast of *The Boys*, reuniting him with *Supernatural* creator Eric Kripke. He is playing the role of Soldier Boy. Together, he and his wife own both the Family Business Brewery in Dripping Springs, Texas; the name is in reference to *Supernatural*, and most recently, they formed Chaos Machine Productions, a deal at Warner Bros. Television.

Ackles is still very active with the *Supernatural* family, as well as You Are Not Alone and other charities such as the JCC (Jacmel

Children's Center in Haiti). Ackles recently collaborated with Jason Manns and other cast members for the Recovering with Friends campaign. It's middle-aged dads singing, and the proceeds go to helping orphans. The Jacmel Children's Center offers a home, education, and a bright future to the orphans of Jacmel. Other cast members on the album include Rob Benedict, Richard Speight Jr., Mark Pellegrino, Kim Rhodes, and Emily Swallow.

And if these guys weren't busy enough, they are all also dads, sharing the love and good times with their kids with all of us, their extended family.

God and Gabriel

Rob Benedict (Chuck/God) and Richard Speight Jr. (Trickster/Gabriel/Loki) also have made their marks on the *Supernatural* family's hearts and impacts in the world through charity work. Richard Speight appeared in *Supernatural* first as what was thought to be a "trickster" type of god, deceiving people's perception of reality for his own pleasure and having a massive sweet tooth to boot. This character was later revealed to be the archangel Gabriel, who just basically got fed up and left heaven, opting for a different life. While the character was only in five episodes from 2007 to 2014, he made a lasting impression on the family. Speight not only acted in episodes but directed many of them as well, enabling him to stay in close contact with current cast members. He made his debut as *Supernatural* director on season 11's episode "Just My Imagination." It was the first episode of the series to be nominated for a Hugo Award. In the season 13 episode "Unfinished Business," Speight not only directed but took on dual acting responsibilities, playing both Loki and Gabriel. He directed a total of eleven episodes from seasons 11 to 15 and is the top eighth director of *Supernatural.*

While Speight has many acting, directing, producing, and singing credits to his name, none of those mean more to me than his charity work with the DAV: Disabled American Veterans, of which my husband is a member.

Speight has been quoted as saying,

> Every day, all over the world, ordinary people do extraordinary things. From defending democracy to delivering humanitarian support. The women and men of our armed forces consistently demonstrate a level of commitment and selflessness that is, to me, awe-inspiring. Regardless of the mission, these people deserve your respect while abroad and our support when they return. That is why I am a proud supporter of the Disabled American Veterans and the work they do for soldiers injured while serving so bravely.

The work of the DAV is very important to our injured veteran's when they come home. Many already facing the mental strain of conflict will now also have to face the long road to recovery, some with even life-changing injuries. All these can be contributing factors to depression and PTSD. The DAV provides free professional help to not only the veteran but their families. They aid in helping them obtain their government benefits and services through military service. Local DAV chapters help veterans with finding housing, paying rent or other bills, and finding employment. The organization is run completely by disabled veterans for disabled veterans, showing a level of compassion that goes above and beyond for their fellow brothers and sisters in arms.

Missouri-born Rob Benedict appeared in *Supernatural* as the character Chuck Shurley, a writer who wrote books that mirrored the boys' lives step by step, word for word. At first thought to be a prophet of the Lord, it was later revealed that he was actually God and had it in for the Winchesters just because they didn't want to play by his rules. Benedict has been involved in stage, film, and television for twenty-five years and has more than seventy acting credits to his name on both TV and screen, but perhaps his biggest role came in 2013, at a *Supernatural* convention where he suffered a stroke. At a Toronto convention while signing autographs, a fan asked him a question, and he suddenly realized he could not speak.

He had no idea what was going on, but not wanting to let his fans down either, he continued the autograph session. Richard, his best friend, came to him when it was done and asked if he wanted to go to dinner with the rest of them. Rob was still unable to speak, and it had become obvious to his friend that something was wrong. Misha then came over and helped Richard realize that something was incredibly wrong and they needed to get Rob to the hospital. Once there, it was realized that his carotid artery had split, causing a blood clot in his brain, which led to aphasia. Doctors gave him a clot-busting shot while in the emergency room. Once realizing how serious the situation was, cast members Richard, Misha, and Jensen all stayed with him that night in the ER and helped to bring his family to Toronto the next day. Benedict stayed a total of ten days in the hospital and took the rest of the year off to focus on recovery. After six months of speech therapy, he was back to playing guitar, singing, and walking—all things doctors said he may never be able to do again.

Rob has made a remarkable recovery and supports the National Stroke Association. The goal of the association is to offer help by reducing the impacts of strokes through educational programs geared at prevention, treatment, support, and rehabilitation for all who have suffered a stroke and their families. As much as 74 percent of all money raised goes to educational purposes alone. While many in the fandom still don't know what happened to Benedict, those who were there still have a hard time talking about it without it bringing tears to their eyes. This definitely brought them all closer together as a family.

The King of Hell, the Demon, and the Witch

From outer space to the underworld and all points in between, London-born Mark Sheppard has had a long career in both movies and television and as a professional musician starting at the age of fifteen, when he began recording and touring with artist and bands including Robyn Hitchcock, the Television Personalities, and the Irish group Light a Big Fire. He was also a session musician and recorded for many groups throughout Europe before eventually moving to the United States.

Sheppard was cast as Crowley the demon, later becoming the King of Hell on *Supernatural* in 2009, first as a recurring character in seasons 5 to 9, and then a regular character in seasons 10 to 12. The smooth-talking, deal-making demon who is always out for himself makes him the perfect foil to the Winchesters.

In reality, though, Mark is about as far away from Crowley as one can get. Mark supports both the Diabetes Research Institute and Camp Conrad Chinnock. These organizations are both designed for helping parents of children with type 1 diabetes, an issue extremely close to Mark's heart as his son Will has type 1 diabetes.

DRIF was started in 1971 by a small group of families with children suffering from diabetes. They came together to support a research program at the University of Miami aimed at finding a cure. The foundation's goal is to provide the Diabetes Research Institute with funding essential to finding a cure for diabetes now.

Camp Conrad Chinnock was started in 1957 when Dr. Robert Chinnock contacted camp director Jim Risner with a proposition of creating a camp for children with type 1 diabetes. The goal was to create a safe camping environment where these children could participate in activities believed only possible for those without. Risner trained and developed staff and programs to include the necessary monitoring and regulation of the children's diabetes. In 1979, Rocky Wilson, PhD became the director of the camp after Risner retired, and he included counseling to help with the psychological issues associated with diabetes. Today the camp is run by the nonprofit organization Diabetic Youth Services.

Rachel Miner is a third-generation actress, daughter of director/producer Peter Miner, and granddaughter of director/producer Worthington Miner and actress Frances Fuller. Miner has been active in film and television since the early '90s and took over the role as the recurring role as demon antagonist Meg Masters on *Supernatural* from 2009 to 2013. The character was filled with devastating sarcasm and normally paired with Castiel, referring to him as Clarence. In 2010, Miner was diagnosed with MS, and in one particular scene with Misha Collins, they were supposed to kiss. He could see that she was having a difficult shoot from the pain she was in, and in an unscripted move, he held her up against the wall while they shared the on-screen moment to help alleviate her pain. Everyone thought, after her diagnosis, she would retire from acting altogether. Quite the opposite has happened in fact; she has become an advocate for actors and actresses with disabilities.

Along with that, she also proudly supports the National MS Society. The organization was founded with the intent of combating multiple sclerosis. The goal of the organization is to provide patients with effective treatment choices and solutions to the challenges of living with this disease. They also push to expand funding and worldwide collaboration to accelerate research. The organization also works to connect those afflicted with MS with others to share support and solutions. They also provide patients with the information and resources needed to combat MS and make fully informed decisions. Along with her support of the MS Society and advocacy work, in September of 2017, Miner became the executive director of Random Acts Inc.

Ruth Connell is a veteran of stage as both an actress and professional dancer/choreographer, performing in many ballets and stage productions. Just like fellow cast mates, she too has had a long career in both television and movies. *Supernatural* fans came to know her as Rowena, the mother to Crowley and everyone's favorite, uh, witch. The red-haired beauty started out as a villain, using her powers of witchcraft against the Winchesters but eventually came to their aid.

Connell's supper power in real life? She is a strong and adamant supporter of the charity My Hope Chest. What is My Hope Chest? It is the only national nonprofit organization whose focus is on underinsured or uninsured breast cancer survivors. The mission is to provide the much-needed closure by helping with reconstructive surgery. My Hope Chest helps all patients who desire to have reconstruction surgery to have it and help them to return to some type of normalcy in their lives. The program that has been created through this charity helps provide reconstruction as soon as possible after a patient has had a mastectomy. The same program also helps educate patients as to what options are available to them, as well as raises public awareness on the need for reconstruction surgery as a means to recovery for underfunded survivors. Not only that, but My Hope Chest educates women about their diagnosis and what to expect and also connects patients with others for support.

Bobby, Jody, and Charlie

Jim Beaver is an actor, playwright, screenwriter, and film historian, but to the *Supernatural* family, he is Bobby Singer, the boys' go-to guy and second father. He is the one who tells Dean, "Family don't end in blood, boy," along with many other memorable one-liners and phrases. Long before his acting career, Beaver served in the military as part of an outlying detachment of the First Marine Regiment near Da Nang, South Vietnam, as a radio operator in 1970. Beaver was discharged from active duty in 1971 and remained in the Marine Reserves until 1976.

While Beaver's acting career has been long and fruitful, his passion and love behind the charity he supports is just as astounding. In 1989, he married his second wife, Cecily Adams, daughter of comic actor Don Adams after four years of dating. Together, the two have a daughter. Sadly, in 2004, Cecily passed away from lung cancer. He wrote a memoir entitled *Life's That Way* in 2003 right after her diagnosis. He also became involved with the John Wayne Cancer Foundation (JWCF) and, as the name implies, it was created to honor John Wayne, who died of stomach cancer. The foundation strives to continue Wayne's passion of helping others combat this horrendous disease. JWCF was established at the John Wayne Cancer Institute at St. John's Health Center located in Santa Monica, California. The research that has taken place at the institute has led to groundbreaking achievements for procedures and treatments in cancers of all types. Beaver has wholeheartedly thrown his support behind this foundation.

Kim Rhodes portrayed Sheriff Jody Mills, first appearing in the season 5 episode "Dead Men Don't Wear Plaid," and her character has appeared in every season since as a guest star. In 2018, the season 13 episode "Wayward Sisters" was used as a backdoor pilot for a possible spin-off series by the same name, intended to feature Rhodes and fellow actresses Briana Buckmaster and Kathryn Newton as the main characters. Ultimately, the new series never progressed forward. For the under-forty crowd, most will remember her from the Disney show *The Suite Life of Zack and Cody* as Carey Martin.

Kim supports many charities, including Ebony Horsewomen Equestrian and Therapeutic Center. The center was founded in 1984 by Patricia E. Kelly, a US Marine Corp Vietnam veteran and African American cowgirl. Patricia had a dream of leveling the playing field so that inner city youth had the same access to opportunities, resources, equine-based programming, and therapy as their suburban counterparts. The EIH offers equine-assisted therapy to adults, children, families, and veterans. It has been proven time and time again that the bond between rider and horse is a very powerful one, and the healing and therapeutic powers of riding helps with PTSD, ADHD, anxiety, and depression.

The EIH has become the regional leader in the provision of equine-assisted therapy and psychotherapy. Kim is also a huge advocate and supporter of the Autistic Self Advocacy Network (ASAN), a nonprofit organization that works toward the advancement of disability rights for people afflicted with autism. Kim, along with her husband, actor Travis Hodges, have a daughter, Tabitha Jane, who is autistic, and in April of 2021, Rhodes herself revealed that she, too, is autistic. The ASAN provides information about autism, disability rights, and system change to the public through a multitude of educational, cultural, and advocacy projects. The ASAN believes that all people with autism have the same rights and opportunities as all other Americans. Their goal is to provide a voice to the autistic community. Kim Rhodes has been quoted as saying, "Nothing about us, without us!" Kim has added her voice to the masses for the rights of all with autism.

Felicia Day is known to *Supernatural* fans as Charlie Bradbury, the tech genius and "little sister" Dean never wanted. So it should be no surprise to fans that Day in real life is also the creator, star, writer and producer of the original web series *The Guild*, a show that was loosely based on her life as a gamer—specifically, an aid gamer. So it should come to no surprise to anyone that the charity she supports is Stomp Out Bullying, one of the leading national anti-bullying and cyberbullying organizations for youth in the US. Since Felicia herself is a major online gamer, combined with the fact that she is famous, she has seen her fair share of online hate and understands what others have experienced. The goal behind the organization is to raise awareness and educate kids, teens, their parents, and even schools about this growing issue. The organization focuses on reducing and stopping all forms of bullying, specifically cyberbullying and other forms of online abuse and hate. The program also provides hope for victims of these harmful actions and teaches both parents and educators how to learn the warning signs of a victim and, most importantly, how to communicate with kids and students. Day believes that all people should come together to combat this growing problem.

The charities and organizations started and supported by the cast members show just how connected they are to their fans and even those who may have never seen one episode. Their ability to give back to the community in various ways is a testament to their humanity. For many of them, the support goes beyond that of monetary giving; these are causes close to their hearts through their own personal experiences and rooted in the need to spread awareness and education and resources for those in need.

CHAPTER 1

My Story

I started this book with the intention of giving a voice to the many fans worldwide who may never have a chance to meet the cast members face to face, myself being one of them, as a giant thank-you to them from the fans for fifteen years of letting us be part of the family. I did not, however, realize the enormous undertaking I had before me when I sent out the call for people to tell me their stories. I thought, maybe if I was lucky, I might get one or two responses and that was it. That wasn't the case; I started receiving messages from people all across the country and from around the world.

You've heard of the butterfly effect? You know the theory that says if a butterfly flaps its wings in one part of the world, it will eventually lead to a massive effect on the other side of the world. Well, I am going to tell you about the Supernatural effect—how one small show caused a worldwide and life-changing experience for its fans.

I am a writer—or at least, I have always fancied myself as one anyway. Who am I? My name is Kellie. I am just a mom and wife who got caught up in the world of a TV show called *Supernatural* and didn't realize that there was an entire subculture surrounding it. Until I started to do the research, I had never heard of AKF or GISH or any of that, and just like with the show itself, I was drawn into these various areas of good works that these organizations do. I was very intrigued by the personal stories the fans had to tell, and a small spark was ignited in my brain. This is my attempt at telling the stories of others, instead of a fictional character. I know there have been other books written and many other stories told, all surrounding the *Supernatural* family cast and fans, and I just want to make some small contribution and acknowledge the cast for their huge impact they have had on the fans over the years.

The idea for this book came to me during all the COVID shutdowns, watching the number of people with depression and anxiety go up and sadly the number of suicides go up as well. I had gone back to writing and dealing with my own health issues and, like everyone else, was bored out of my freaking mind. I started writing a *Supernatural* fan fiction and was sitting at my laptop one night when that small spark became a raging fire. This was the result of big dreams, a passion to help people anyway that I could, and taking a chance. I began by asking people to tell me how the show had impacted their own personal lives. It was a very, very slow start, which is understandable, but once I started talking to people, it took off like a house on fire.

I'm one of those *Supernatural* fans who was late to the party. You might say I hadn't followed the show from the very beginning and had only been a fan since 2019, when my youngest daughter introduced me to it. And just like everyone else you will read about, I was hooked; however, I wasn't able to watch on a regular basis at first due to extreme family issues I had to deal with. Mental health issues such as PTSD, depression, anxiety, self-harm, and suicide prevention are all issues I am very passionate about—a passion that comes from being on both sides of the mirror as it were. I am a suicide survivor, and as you will see, I have battled many demons, as have many of the fans I have interviewed.

I want to bring mental illness out of the shadows and help people to understand that it can affect anyone at any time, any age, any race, or any gender. It doesn't discriminate, and neither should we as a society. Depression and anxiety aren't something that we who are affected by it can just turn on and off when we feel like it, but there is good news out there. There are people out in this crazy world who truly care and truly want to help. And to me, if this book reaches just one person and gives them hope and helps them to find the light at the end of what can seem like a never-ending dark tunnel, then I have accomplished something. Either way, talking to the people I talked to and making the lifelong friends and connections that I have made is worth everything to me.

I really don't know where to start when it comes to myself to be honest. I grew up the oldest daughter of three. My mom, a stay-at-home mom and perfect parent to the outside world, was an alcoholic and a perfectionist. We lived in a museum—not that there's anything wrong with a clean house, but ours looked more like a display home than a home with kids in it. I had toys for play and toys for display at the time that didn't make any sense. My father, a Vietnam veteran, was a workaholic and tried to be there as much as he could but wasn't. I grew up being the tomboy, oddball, having low self-esteem and body-image problems before I even hit puberty. I was constantly wanting to be under cars, in the mud, or doing what the boys were doing—not an ideal situation for my mom who was trying to raise prim and proper ladies.

I dealt with a constant barrage of insults from my mother pointing out several of my flaws. I am the child of adoption and was once even told how she wished they had never adopted me. Most of this occurred when she was intoxicated, and all of the time I was made to feel as if it were all my fault. As I got older, the insults became physical: being dragged out of bed by my hair, having my nose bloodied, and a board broken over my head, just to name a few. I took it all, feeling the need to protect my younger siblings. Now, I'll admit I wasn't a perfect angel, but I wasn't a demon either. I was just a kid doing kid things, and those kid things elicited an overreaction from my mother, who I believe was a victim of abuse herself but has never denied nor confirmed my thoughts.

At thirteen, my family was hit hard as I was diagnosed with epilepsy. The doctors were unsure what the cause of it was—whether it was a hormonal shift or something else like a head trauma. Feeling the need to somehow protect my abuser when asked if I had ever been hit in the head, I just told the doctors I fell off my skateboard once and knocked my head off the concrete. This was in the time before helmets were an essential part of outside gear when bike riding or skateboarding. I was placed on an array of medications that first summer, along with doctor visits and blood workups, all which annoyed my mother. I remember being looked at like I was some type of fragile doll by many people when I went back to school.

The older I got, the deeper and deeper I fell into a depressive state. Writing and music were my only outlets to deal with. I dreamed of one day being a musician or a writer or both. The solitude of my basement room or "cave," as it came to be known, was both my blessing and curse. There I was free to dream and imagine a life where I was free from abuse and hurtful words and the stench of addiction. Then night would fall, and my demons came out to play in my head, reaffirming everything my mother had ever told me, telling me I was useless, nobody would ever love me, just end it all. At fifteen, I made my first attempt at suicide by slashing my wrist; it wasn't deep enough that I needed to go to the hospital—that or I missed the vein completely. However, had it been a successful attempt, no one would have found me until the next morning. I didn't even leave a note and did my best to conceal the cut so my mother wouldn't make fun of me for that.

In May of 1995, my father had a massive heart attack at work and was placed on life support for two weeks before we let him go. The whole time he was there my mother felt the need to lie to all of us as to what was going on. It was two days before she told me what had happened, and she let me go with her.

Unfortunately for her, I wasn't stupid. I knew something bad had happened. Too many people were calling our house, and when she came home that night, this normally pristine-looking woman looked like she had been put through the wringer. When the decision was finally made to take him off of life support and he passed away, she waited till 11:30 that night to tell me and my middle sister because he passed away the day of her eighth grade graduation. To this day, I have really tried to understand my mom's logic on this; however, she was also of the thinking that if you just ignored a problem long enough, it would just go away on its own too.

Once again my demons rose up in me. How was I going to get through now with my dad gone? He may not have been around a lot, but when he was, he was my biggest supporter and actually understood my weird sense of humor. Once again suicide crossed my mind. I was going to drive my car into a guardrail and down an embankment; I had it all planned out. I started to pick up speed down the two-lane highway out of the small town I lived in. As I took my hands off the wheel, my eyes filled with tears as I felt the car start to veer the way I wanted it to go. I closed my eyes and relaxed. At the last moment, something stopped me inches from the guardrail; maybe something in my brain just clicked and said I wasn't going out like this. I don't know.

Regardless, my senior year of high school was very hard on me as I had become very withdrawn. For classes that were normally a breeze for me like music, history, and English, I was failing and failing these miserably, which prompted teachers and counselors alike to attempt to reach out to Mom to no avail. She believed it was all an act, and I was just looking for sympathy and attention. Everything finally came to a head between her and me in the fall of 1996. I had been in college for about a month and dating my "high school sweetheart." I don't even remember now what the fight was over, but it was a big one, and I packed my stuff and left, moving in with my boyfriend. My stubborn side took over, and I showed her attitude. She figured in a week tops, I would be gone. I was gone ten months before that all went to hell, and I needed to come back with my tail tucked between my legs. I was allowed to only after she came back from a two-week vacation, leaving me homeless for two weeks. I was sleeping on couches, living out of a trash bag full of clothes, sometimes not even knowing where or who I was going to stay with.

Moving back home was fine for a little while, until the epilepsy showed its ugly head again. I worked at our local pizza restaurant as a manager and had a seizure while working a birthday party for a friend of Mom. My mom was embarrassed; I lost my job over it. And again I had a seizure while my youngest sister and I were swimming in our pool, and they had to pull me out. After I had fully recovered from it, my mom came to me telling me she couldn't take care of me and "this seizure thing," as she put it. She thought the best place for me was an assisted living center. That's a very hard pill to swallow when your mother tells you to look into an assisted living center. I have grand mal seizures—that's it—and at that point in time, they weren't under control. I stayed with my mom for a few more months and one night came home from my waitressing job at a local diner to find both of my sisters in the kitchen with heartbroken looks on their faces. My middle sister handed me a note from our mom; it basically said she was throwing me out. She didn't even have the courage to tell me to my face, which is probably what hurts the most to this day. That's one thing about me—at least I speak the truth, good, bad, or indifferent. It may not be what someone wants to hear at the time, but it's probably something they need to hear, and I always do it face to face. I don't hide behind a screen or text or a piece of paper.

Not knowing what else to do, I called a good friend I met in college, and he gave me a place to stay as long as I needed. My plan was to find a job and save money for a car and a place of my own and go back to living my life the way I wanted to. Well, fate had other plans, so to speak.

My friend ended up being my now husband of twenty years as of June 2020, Marty. It wasn't a whirlwind romance by any means, but it was different. Like I said, I met Marty in college. I was eighteen, and he was thirty-one—yes, I said thirty-one; he is thirteen years older than me. He was there on a veteran's grant as he is a Desert Storm-era veteran. He jokes and always tells everyone he fell in love with my big toe. It was still summer and I was wearing sandals, and he looked down and saw my painted toenails, and he claimed by the time he made it to my knee, he was in love. I know...*awww.*

By all accounts, we should have failed from the start, and I'm sure psychologists would have a field day trying to figure out how we managed to stay together as long as we have. Aside from the age difference, we are total opposites when it comes to pretty much everything. We grew up in two totally different socioeconomic classes. He's the youngest of thirteen kids who grew up poor, and I'm the oldest of three who grew up in a middle-class family. Somehow though we both managed to make it work, we both had demons that haunted us daily. Marty suffers from PTSD from not only his time in the service but from other childhood traumas, along with depression and anxiety. You know the saying "misery loves company"? That was us for a while, until his PTSD became almost unbearable for me to handle. Like I said, my father was also a veteran; his way of dealing was to work himself to death. Marty's way of dealing was at times bad dreams and sometimes narcissistic personality and violent mood swings that came out of nowhere where he would just leave instead of taking it out on me. However, it still didn't stop me from feeling guilty like I had somehow provoked it.

We married in June of 2000, and our first child, Victoria, was born in February of 2001—despite warnings from doctors that I shouldn't even attempt to try to carry a child due to the fact that my epilepsy wasn't under control; in fact, the first obstetrician we saw even recommended that I have an abortion because my child could have been born with all sorts of birth defects or learning disabilities. Truth be told, both of my daughters are both highly intelligent and talented in various areas. Neither one of them has ever exhibited any signs of any type of learning disorders.

Since I had totally thrown my mother's guide to being a mom out the window when my first child was born, I pretty much made the rules up as I went along, not wanting to fall into the trap of being like my mom. Our second daughter, Jamie, was born in March of 2004, and I had suffered miscarriages between them and after my youngest—a total of three altogether. Life with two children three years apart, a husband who is not only trying to work and provide for his family but who is also suffering from his traumatic experiences, and me dealing with constant seizures was no picnic to say the least. Our children, of course, were always our first priority, and as I couldn't work, I was able to stay home in those early years and focus on them.

I decided to let them find themselves at an early age. If they wanted to wear the hot pink shirt with the blue pants and mismatched socks, I wasn't going to stop them. I wasn't going to squash their confidence because they thought out of the box like I did. This is probably why today one daughter has blue hair and one has purple, but then again I have violet hair. I tried very hard to keep my demons at bay while they were growing up and concentrate on being a good mom and wife.

Eventually, doctors got me on the right combination of medication, and the seizures subsided for years to nothing more than occasional body jerks. My husband and I started a business that we ran together for eleven years and were successful at it, even moving from Illinois, the state where both of us were born and raised, to Missouri to just have a fresh start in life. Things had really started to look up for us, and that's normally when the other shoe drops.

There were still many hard times after Marty and I married. On top of everything else, he was also addicted to gambling—more specifically, poker. Marty is the youngest of three boys and has always lived in the shadow of his two older brothers. So to compensate and to try to make them proud, as his father was absent and died when he was ten, he always tried to be just as good or better than them at the same things they excelled in. This, for one thing, isn't healthy, and two, everyone has their own unique qualities. Marty's middle brother was an absolute genius on the poker table, even making it all the way to the World Series of Poker and making it to the cash prize part, though he didn't make it to the final table. Marty had the same dreams—just not the same type of cash, using our bill money to play in local tournaments. Sometimes he would win; other times he would leave us to rob Peter to pay Paul, and always he would say he could stop anytime he wanted, causing lots of unwanted and unnecessary stress and anxiety in our marriage.

In 2017, my husband of seventeen years started having strange and extreme health issues other than just the PTSD and the anxiety and depression—but these were problems to the extent of needing blood transfusions almost every other week, and the doctors couldn't explain why. On a date I will never forget, July 27, 2017, we were getting ready to take him to the hospital when he collapsed. The ambulance came and took him to Cape Girardeau, Missouri. I left my then-sixteen-year-old and thirteen-year-old daughters at home, thinking we would be home later that evening. When I arrived at the hospital, they didn't take me back immediately to see him, and when I was allowed to go back, he had all sorts of tubes and IVs running out of him. The doctor informed me that not only was he in congestive heart failure, his kidneys were failing him, and his entire body was beginning to shut down. They were getting ready to transfer him to the ICU so they could start dialysis on him and monitor his heart, and different specialists were being called in.

All the while he was awake and began to have a panic attack, which caused his already-weak body to code. I ran out of the ICU all the while hearing "Code blue ICU." No one was there with me but ten thousand fears attacking me all at once—the worst ones. Here I sat in a cold hospital hallway while doctors worked to keep my husband alive, and I'm letting these fears creep in. I was only thirty-nine years old at the time. My husband and I had run a small business at the time. I began to panic. What if he died? How was I going to keep our business going and take care of our daughters?

Finally, after what seemed like an eternity, the nurse came and got me. They had gotten him stable, and he was on a ventilator. They told me there was really nothing else they could do at that point, and I should go home to my children. I tried to pull myself together the best I could for them, praying they would be asleep when I walked in the door as it was almost two in the morning when I did. They weren't, and they saw right through me. I had no choice but to be honest with them mainly because it was the right thing to do, but also because I made a promise the day I found out I was pregnant with Victoria that no matter how bad the situation was, I would always be honest with my kids, unlike my own mom.

29

As hard as it was going to be for me to tell my girls what was going on, I knew it was going to be even harder on them. They were going to need me, and my mother's tactic of ignoring the problem wasn't going to help them. I walked in that house that night and saw two pairs of brown eyes looking to me for answers—some I had, some I didn't, but regardless, I had to be the one to stand up and take on the responsibility now. No matter how bad or how dark things were about to get for us, we would face it together as a family.

After a few days my husband came off the ventilator, he was completely paralyzed on his left side, and no one knew why. The doctors kept telling me that he hadn't had a stroke, and they were dumbfounded as to his condition. He endured many painful tests—everything from bone marrow tests to spinal taps; they were looking for anything.

After months—yes, I said months—of switching him from hospital to hospital, my girls and I had to stay with friends because the landlord we had at the time threw us out after believing I wouldn't be able to pay our rent. I fell into a deep depression once again, but still somehow, I kept pushing myself to the brink of both mental and physical exhaustion. Other than a small handful of friends and my girls, I really had no one to help me, and now I was thrown into the role of both mother and father, provider and protector, and all major decisions were now laid at my doorstep where they had always been both me and my husband's. The seizures had caused me to go from a nerdy, outgoing, socially awkward jokester to a shy, still socially awkward wallflower. With my husband now sick, it was time for the shy Kellie to go away and find that outgoing kid again, but I was too afraid for a long time, so I faked it for a while.

Throughout that entire period, I had plenty of people tell they couldn't believe how strong I was, and they didn't think they could handle all that I had handled. I had two choices: lay down and stay down or get up every day and push through.

Finally, a tiny silver lining started to appear. I moved myself and my girls into a home, my husband was finally moved to a skilled care facility where he could get the care he needed, and I found a job so I could be more accessible to my children. However, like clouds have a tendency to do, my gray skies returned. Some days were just that gray, other days brought rain, and others brought storms I didn't think I would survive. I waited till late at night to break down, never letting my girls see me cry, always appearing to be their rock, their shoulder, the one they could depend on. But like all rocks under pressure, I broke. It happened when my youngest daughter came one night and told me that one day, while her sister and I were both gone, a guy she had thought was a friend came to my house and stole her innocence. He had raped her in *my house!* I saw red. The walls fell down around me. I had failed my child. I hadn't protected her. I had broken my promise to her.

I went through every legal avenue I knew to go through to have the animal locked away—to no avail because my daughter had waited too long to report it. Then came the unending torture she dealt with at school because no one believed this person could have done this, and my daughter must have made it up. I knew all the pain she was suffering and dealing with because I myself am a rape and abuse survivor. However, she just shut down, sinking further and further into the depths of depression, contemplating self-harm, and ultimately suicide. Thankfully, though, she never carried out with either.

Where I am a writer and express myself through that form, she is an exceptional artist, and she draws and paints her feelings to get them out. She had already dealt with the death of an uncle she was very close to and her father being taken away and now this trauma— all back to back to back; even for an adult, that's a lot to tackle. She had a hard time opening up to me because she knew all my stress and didn't want to burden me any further. She found *Supernatural* thanks to a very good friend and started talking about it and explaining it all to me. So the gears in my brain began to turn. I thought, if I started watching the show myself, that would give us a common ground, something we could both talk about. And I did for a while, and then life caught back up with me—jobs, bills, my own health. I had only made it through the first two seasons before I had to stop watching, but the show was never far from my mind.

Regarding a lot of the show's main principles, I have lived by these most of my life. I have friends who are family to me, and no one will ever tell me any different. I am able to relate with Dean on many levels. I am the oldest child and would go to hell and back not only for my siblings but for my children as well. I give no care to myself; I am always worried about everyone around me, but if anyone asks how I'm doing, it's always "I'm fine." I've always considered myself a coward for the most part, but the last several years have brought a new aspect to my personality, and I have come to the point that if someone is coming after my family, they have to go through me and I'll go down swinging.

I can also relate to Castiel as well. Some days I have an over-abundance of faith, and I always want to do what's right. I always think from my heart and not my head, which can get me into trouble at times, and I am very, very socially awkward. Over the last year, I have been able to get back to watching the show due to the fact I have started having problems with my epilepsy again. After going years without a seizure, I started having them, and I have also started having back and hip problems at the time of me writing this. I am waiting to have SI infusions on both sides and waiting on seeing a specialist in St. Louis for a second opinion on my MRI. So between COVID and my own issues, I've had plenty of time. I began following different fan groups on social media and got involved with GISH and Random Acts, as well as learning as much as I could about AKF. I am even part of an AKF support group on Facebook and have my own little "battle buddy." It's a stuffed companion that looks like a moose in reference to a nickname given to Jared's character, Sam, but the purpose of the battle buddy is to have something with you during the good and bad times. Mine is watching me right now while I'm writing.

If you are a fan and even if you are not and you are reading this, I highly recommend also getting involved with GISH and Random Acts. They both do so much good in a world full of so much pain and turmoil. I know that it totally restored my faith in humanity altogether. I not only played in the mini hunts but was involved in the card exchanges at Christmas time, and I received cards from all over the world. I have a pen pal in Australia, and we get to learn about each other and our two totally different cultures—it is so amazing.

And I wouldn't have gotten involved with any of this had it not been for a little show called *Supernatural*.

If I had one wish, it would be that I could attend an actual in-person convention when they start having them again, just so I could tell the cast, "Thank you. Thank-you for the impact you have had, the lives you have saved, and the families you have created where there were once strangers. The reach of *Supernatural* goes far beyond the show, far beyond the actors themselves. We are all truly a family."

I thoroughly believe that most people really don't take the time to really think about how mental health affects people until maybe we see something like a tragic suicide of an actor or musician. Then, for a little while, everyone jumps on the bandwagon while it's fashionable or trending, then just as quickly, it fades away. The ugly truth is we lose twenty-two veterans a day to suicide—read that again. Twenty-two servicemen and women per day to suicide, men and women who served this country. And the VA has a resource line for them, but it's still not enough.

Since the COVID lockdowns, the CDC reported that they found elevated levels of symptoms of anxiety and depressive disorders, substance use, and suicidal ideation among US adults and identified populations at risk, including young people, racial and ethnic minorities, essential workers, and caregivers of adults. More than 20 percent of our essential workers reported suicidal thoughts, while 75 percent of our young people have reported at least one adverse mental health symptom. The respondents were in the age group of eighteen-to-twenty-four-year-olds, and of that 75 percent, 25 percent had thoughts of suicide. So to me this isn't something that just quickly trends and fades away. These are our loved ones, our friends, family, coworkers. I've lost close friends to suicide and watch many more suffer with different issues due to the lack of empathy from people who believe depression is just about being sad and they have nothing to be sad about. Yes, this is about how a TV show saved my life and the lives of others, but it's only because the people involved with that show took a stand and said, "No more!" Just like I am taking a stand now.

I'm not in this for fame or notoriety. I'm here to give a voice to the voiceless and to say, "I am here, no matter what." If these words and stories can reach just one person, then to me it's been worth it—all the pain and struggles that I have gone through to come out on the other side into the arms of a family not bound by blood. I proudly wear the AKF tattooed on my right shoulder as a conversation starter along with the semicolon over the scar on my left wrist. I am no longer ashamed of who I was; it is those scars that made me.

My past didn't defeat me or define me, but it did teach me. I had no one to turn to in the darkest moments of my life. I truly believed God hated me and that I was truly alone. I could have very easily retreated and ended my own story and left the pages blank and family and friends wondering what I could have become. I could have left them all scratching their heads wondering why I never told them what was wrong. I didn't. I kept pushing and praying for something or someone out there to understand what I was feeling, what I was going through. I found that in the world of *Supernatural*, human characters with flaws are portrayed by humans with hearts and the willingness to share and give back.

Their passion turned my spark to help others into a raging inferno. I want to give a voice to the voiceless and let others know, not just the fans, that there are people who are willing to listen. You are not alone, and you don't have to suffer in silence or embarrassment, and it's okay to lean on someone and to reach out for help. That's my wish for you, the reader, if you are suffering with any type of anxiety, depression, suicidal ideations. I encourage to please reach out to your local agencies for assistance or please call the national suicide hotline at 800-273-8255.

If you are a veteran in crisis, please call 855-968-0965.

You can also find many resources online and on social media as well. Our stories are far from over; in fact, some of them are just beginning.

> Hey, sweetheart, I know life throws a crap load
> of bullshit and sometimes all you want to do is
> give up. I want you to know, there's a light at the

end of the tunnel. Even if it takes days, months, or even years, I promise I will make damn sure you get everything you deserve. Don't stop fighting. You're a Winchester and you know us, we never give up. We kick ass and move forward. Sammy and I love you. And we will always be here for you. Keep your head, kiddo.

—Dean Winchester

CHAPTER 2

Kristy's Story

Kristy's story is very interesting and without a doubt a testament to the power of the *Supernatural* family. When I asked for volunteers to be interviewed, Kristy was one of the first ones to get in touch with me, though without her reservations. And rightfully so. There are so many scams running rampant on social media; it was completely understandable that she was skeptical of my intentions. She reached out to me, and we began to talk and found we had more in common than just *Supernatural*, even with a seventeen-year age difference and two thousand miles separating us. We found kindred spirits in each other. According to Kristy, she really had nothing better to do than look at Facebook because she was stuck at home with COVID, which is when she saw the post and was also curious as to what I was looking for. We began talking, and I explained the idea for the book and told her a little bit about myself, and things just took off from there.

Kristy began watching the show in 2015 because of her fiancé, though she admits he had a hard time getting her to watch it at first because of some of the subject matter that touches on God and angels. From her early childhood through her early twenties, she was the victim of mental, physical, and other abuses throughout her life. All of her hope was gone, and she just wanted to escape all of it desperately, even if it meant taking her own life. She just truly wanted to forget any of it ever happening at any cost. She was struggling mentally and was in a bad situation where she feared harm, and she had begun watching *Supernatural*, which provided her a positive form of escape. The values spoken on the show started to impact the way she viewed life. The most important thing—and she says the silliest thing perhaps—is that the show and the cast and characters have made her smile and laugh, and she cannot explain how thankful she is for that. That one little happy moment meant everything to her, and the impact was so strong that it stopped her from self-harm and possibly worse at times. She later began watching the clips of the conventions on YouTube as a way to find out more about *Supernatural*. She says she was truly shocked in a good way. She thinks that the cast are all amazing people who in her opinion generally care about their fans and each other. And it doesn't hurt that the cast are a little crazy and know how to have fun, especially Misha!

Kristy was very surprised to see over and over again the cast's caring nature with the fans and their interactions with them. She later learned more about all of them and their specific charities like You Are Not Alone, which is a very important message to her as she personally struggles with major depression, anxiety, and PTSD on a daily basis. She found herself being able to relate with the different cast members on a more personal level; for instance, Misha Collins, who as a youth struggled with homelessness and never let it defeat or define him. He became successful and uses that to help others through his various charity works.

Kristy herself also had to deal with homelessness as a youth on multiple occasions due to her mother's poor choices, then later again to escape abusive and dangerous housemates, and she refused to let it define her or break her. She has a deep respect for the cast, which is an important thing to her seeing as how she never really thought much about who made movies or TV shows other than thinking it was a really cool job to have. With *Supernatural*, she says it's not hard to get sucked into the unstoppable tide of jokes and laughter they radiate. She says if she ever has the chance to talk to them, she wants to let them all know how important they are and that they really have made a difference in her life. She really wants to thank them for that and for every smile that she cracked and every time she laughed so hard she couldn't breathe at the positive effect it had on her. She would especially just like to say thank you for just being who they are and hopes they never change.

Kristy's life is better now. Though she does still struggle from time to time with her mental health, things aren't as dark as they once were. And she can always watch *Supernatural* or the cast being funny on YouTube, and it cheers her up most of the time.

Kristy and I have continued to stay in contact in the months since her interview. We found a common ground not only in being fans of the show but in so many other facets of our lives. We talk to each other nearly every day, sometimes two or three times a day, just to check on each other. We have found inspiration in each other and become the voice in the other's head saying, "It's okay, I believe in you!" When we first started talking, we found out we were both working on our own versions of fan fictions. I had been writing mine as a way to just cure the boredom and as a way to deal with the depression I was sometimes feeling. Kristy was writing a Dungeons and Dragons game she plays with both her husband and a friend.

Shortly after we started getting to know each other, we began sharing our work with each other and eventually incorporated our characters into our stories. Not only have we shared our fictional stories with each other, but we have shared our own personal lives with each other, becoming a long-distance family of sorts. We send each other packages, as she is also an artist and extremely crafty with her hands. I can't craft and I can barely draw, but I manage to find things I know she is interested in and send them to her. Our goal is to eventually meet each other face to face, either by my family going to California or she and her husband coming to Missouri or just all of us meeting halfway.

She has literally become the Sam to my Dean, another sister to me that I would have never known had it not been for *Supernatural*.

There is no doubt in my mind that other friendships have been forged this way too. I am so very honored to call Kristy my friend, and she calls me the same. Though our struggles are so very different, the reality for us is identical. The stigma that shrouds depression and anxiety and PTSD does more harm to those who suffer from it, making it hard for those who need help to reach out and ask.

For those who don't suffer from it, they think it's like a light switch that we can just turn on and off—and it's not. The overwhelming feelings that hit you like a ton of bricks make it impossible to get out of bed some days. When added with other physical health problems, it can be crippling almost to the point you want to completely shut down and shut yourself away from everyone. I have seen it happen, and I have been the one to do it also.

Since I met Kristy, we both now have someone in our corner to give us that extra little push we need on a daily basis, not just our close family. I firmly believe without *Supernatural*, without the closeness of the fan base, and without such things as AKF, we never would have met. For some it might not be the ideal set up for a friendship and certainly back in the day, before mobile phones and the Internet, it would have gotten very expensive to talk every night on the phone, considering she's in California and I'm in Missouri— but we make it work. And it helps that our personalities mesh well together too. We can both be a little on the crazy side at times. My kids say when they hear us talking on the phone, it sounds like two teenage girls laughing and giggling over silly things. Oh well, such is life.

A note from Kristy: the reason I'm able to put this note is because I read and edited her book. Basically, I give Kellie my opinion and spell-check as I read in case she missed something. Now on to how that happened in the first place...

I met Kellie rather unexpectedly through *Supernatural.* I was browsing and found a post asking for interviews on how the show affected your life. I was curious, but I felt like perhaps this was a scam of some form and if it was not the thought of opening up to someone was hard, so I thought about it a few days then shot her a message asking if she had interest in interviewing me. She did and we started to talk, and I noticed something as we texted back and forth—this woman had shared a lot of the same pain I had and understood how I felt as well as being genuinely caring. This in its own way made it so I felt comfortable in opening up to her, and I decided to tell her some of the things I had been through hoping that if the book was ever published that someone would read my story and feel like they were not alone in this cruel world. I understand how they feel. I have been through similar situations as they have or you the reader has, and I have survived. It may not seem like it at times, but you can make it through the pain, so never stop fighting, you are worth it. A second thing I was hoping to express is my heartfelt gratitude to the cast for smiles that sometimes made all the difference in the world on days I was scared, depressed, or both.

This initial idea turned into something far more through our talks that became more and more frequent and long. I had found a true friend that I feel will last a lifetime or longer, and if not for *Supernatural*'s existence, and if not for that group being there as a way for people to connect,

I would've never met her. She did not care how awkward I was, how weird I think I am, or any of the other flaws I have. None of it mattered to her, and that meant a lot to me.

Kellie and I spend a good deal of time laughing about things like the characters' J2M pranks, and for those who don't know what that is, look it up—you won't be disappointed. My personal favorite is the story about the pennies in Jared's trailer and Misha's car—it puts a whole new spin on the word *payback*.

Additionally, I have found myself pranking Kellie and will randomly put the word *pineapples* in somewhere while I'm editing to see if she finds it, which she has every time so far, but if you see that out-of-context word, you will know how it got there.

Anyway Kellie and I have become very good friends and at times I was upset. I have been able to talk with her and vice versa. She is there when I need her, and I want to be there for her too. She has also gotten me into writing not just my D&D plots but now fanfic, which I never did before, and other stories as well. We also read each other's work, even combining it at times.

"Family don't end in blood" could not be a truer statement. Kellie is my family, and I love her like a sister. I even talk with her daughters now who are both amazing and caring people. I'm so happy to have met her, and I don't even have the words to express how much I appreciate her. (Kristy, California)

It's just people trying to do their best in a world where it is far too easy to do your worst.
—Castiel/Misha Collins

CHAPTER 3

Michael's Story

I found myself realizing as I spoke to all of these people that they are all very unique individuals, with all very different stories to tell, with one common theme of course. They found either solace, comfort, strength, or all these within the fictional world of *Supernatural*, mainly because of how relatable the characters are—granted I don't think any of us are just going to give up our day jobs and drive around with our sibling or best friend going across the country getting rid of monsters, ghosts and demons. That's not what I mean when I said the characters are relatable, but hey who knows, you got to do what moves you, right?

The human, everyday realistic drama and drive that exists between and with the main characters of Dean and Sam Winchester is what makes them that way. The normal, everyday survival and struggle of these two are enough: Dean's overprotectiveness of Sam, Sam's empathy, their need for answers. The paranormal stories intrigue us, the human stories touch us and make us root for them.

In Michael's case, he has been a fan since the show first aired in 2005, with Sam being the character he relates to the most. He says he was immediately hooked and has always been a fan of paranormal stories, so the show was right up his alley. Watching the whole storyline start to unfold from the very beginning and using the plot device of having Dean say, "Dad's on a hunting trip and hasn't been home in a few days." Pulling Sam back into the family business has grabbed Michael hook, line, and sinker. Michael adores Dean, and that specific character has probably tugged on his heartstrings more than anyone else. However, he easily identifies with Sam and some of his struggles.

He doesn't necessarily have a favorite character; however, Castiel is just adorable, the socially awkward angel. He absolutely loathed Rowena (Ruthie Connell) when she first appeared but claims that she was an excellent character, so wicked. Over time he came to love as she started to work with the boys instead of against them. Another character on his love-to-hate list has to be Lucifer (Mark Pellegrino). Michael said he never found anything redeeming about the character at all. Was he funny and sarcastic? Yes, but come on, I mean it's Lucifer. Is there really supposed to be anything redeeming about him? "Sam Interrupted" (S5 E11) is by far the most meaningful episode to Michael. He explained it to me this way: he is much more than just a casual fan watching the series (with the exception of season 15) a total of seven different times. He has merchandise from the show and claims there isn't a day that goes by where *Supernatural* isn't involved in his life.

He had cancer when he was sixteen, and the chemo left him messed up with a lot of long-term side effects: some physical scars but far more emotional and mental ones. He was diagnosed with depression in 2007 and started taking prescription medication that same year. He claims he was obviously not "content" with taking responsibility for his own happiness, so he allowed himself to become a prisoner of his own mind with lots of ups and downs and several thoughts of suicide. Finally hitting rock-bottom in July of 2020, he says that's when *Supernatural* saved his life. His anxiety over the years and with COVID and lockdowns in full effect had caused him to become withdrawn from pretty much everyone outside his family. He had social anxiety to the point he rarely ever left his house, and then just anxiety over other things. It was becoming a vicious, tortuous cycle—plus the medication always made him tired.

In August of 2020, he watched "Sam Interrupted," and according to Michael, the speech that Sam gives at the end hit him much differently despite his seeing the episode several times. He just broke down into tears. It was at that moment everything changed for him. He began taking things in his life more seriously, like his diet for one. At the time of this interview, he was down 108 pounds. He began taking better care of his overall health and appearance. He had talked for the last fifteen years about buying the clear braces to fix his teeth, and after years of talk, he finally got them. He also finally realized and accepted the fact that no one can make him happy but himself. He began to cut ties with toxic people from his life and change his outlook on everything. He's looking to make even bigger changes in the future, including moving from his home state of Florida and living a life of his own. He says the most uncharacteristic thing he's planning on doing is taking a Winchester-style road trip with his dad, taking backroads, sleeping in cheap motels and roadside dinners, just seeing America.

His personal message to the cast and crew is simply thank you. "Thank you for the wonderful world you created for all of us to lose ourselves in and be a part of. Your blood, sweat, tears, hard work, struggles, and sacrifices are appreciated more than any of you could ever know.

"It wasn't just a TV show you made possible. You made a family, and you have touched so many lives in so many ways."

The Winchesters have been a part of Michael's life far longer than all but one of his friendships, and he always wanted brothers, so to him, Dean and Sam will be as close as he will ever come, and they will forever hold a place in his heart.

The final season was met with high emotion by cast, crew, and fans alike. The series finale was due to air in May 2020; however, due to COVID, the show went on hiatus in March 23, 2020, leaving many fans like Michael questioning, How will it end? Will it do the show justice? Finally, after what seemed like a lifetime, filming resumed in August of 2020 with full COVID restrictions in place.

The night the final episode aired, Michael says he sent out a message to let everyone know he would be off of his phone and watching it. Like all of us, for him it was beyond emotionally gut-wrenching. He was fully expecting one of them to die but was not prepared for how it would affect him. It was like a member of his own family had just died. He believes that the final episode was done perfectly and gave both of the boys the send-off we always knew they would have. Dean went out the way he always said he would—in the middle of a hunt—and Sam went on to eventually live a long life and have a family, only to be reunited with Dean in heaven.

Well, what more can anyone ask for? Michael, again I want to thank you for sharing your story with me, and I wish you the best of luck in all your future endeavors. From one wayward child to another, always keep fighting!

> We are all humans doing our best. No one
> is better than anybody else. We are all just
> here, we all have struggles and strengths.
> —Jared Padalecki

CHAPTER 4

Desiree's Story

I met Desiree in one of the Facebook mental health support groups. She is the administrator for the You Are Not Alone or YANA group, along with a few others. It is based on Collins's and Ackles's message that no one is alone and addresses mental health issues and offers support to its members. They also do daily check-ins and offer a safe space where people do not have to fear judgement for their feelings. While no one in the group is a licensed therapist, they do offer resources to those who are in critical need. And just knowing that someone is there to listen and talk to twenty-four hours a day makes a huge difference. I would like to personally thank Desiree for being so open and candid with me in sharing her story.

Desiree became a fan at the very start. When she first saw the show, she had been admitted to a mental health ward for suicidal ideations. While she was there, *Supernatural* came on the TV in the common room; she had never heard of it and decided to watch. And just like everyone else, she was hooked with one line: "Whoa, easy tiger…" And bam, she was in love.

She identifies the most with Dean, saying a lot of her personality is identical to his—the good and the bad. Desiree says that she can have a very sarcastic attitude at times while being fiercely protective of her family and friends. As the show progressed and the character of Dean grew, matured, and faced many trials, she also began to identify more and more with sacrifice and how caring he was toward others, yet he felt this huge sense of worthlessness and saw himself as nothing. That's how Desiree had always felt and seeing a character portrayed as having those same emotions really hit her hard.

Desiree had attempted suicide on different occasions. When Jared came out and started talking openly about his own battles with depression and showing that it was okay to ask for help, that there was no shame in being weak, it opened her eyes. She realized that she needed help and sought it out. And that is what helped her to find her true calling in helping others by volunteering and eventually starting YANA. She uses her own experiences to help others.

The actors' own personal stories have taught her a lot about how to look at her own life, how to be an all-around better person, and lead a life of kindness and love, leaving hatred and anger at the door. She credits Ackles and Collins for her group is still around; their message of You Are Not Alone really resonates with her, and she truly believes in it. In the Facebook family, no is alone, and there are so many reaching out for help and a safe place to find it.

Had it not been for *Supernatural,* Desiree may not even be here today because the cycle of feeling alienated may have continued, and she may have never reached out for the help she desperately needed. In turn, she has been able to help others the way she has and gained not only a family she never had but friends she never would have met. The show taught her that family is so much more than blood and what love and sacrifice really mean. The show teaches us so many lessons.

Her message to Jared and Jensen is simply…

> Thank you, guys! You don't even know the amount of lives you've saved by portraying Sam and Dean Winchester and for being the great men that you are. You have truly inspired people to keep going even during the worst moments of their lives. You have shown that with dedication and fight you can make your dreams come true. You have both overcome obstacles and stood by each other during the difficult and the good times. You led me down a path that truly helped other people. Your kindness is what could save the world if we allow it. If just one person helps another and that person helps three, the *Supernatural* family will spread far and wide. The message that family doesn't end in blood and we will stick together through everything because we are family will go on. Desiree loves you guys more than you will ever know, please never change. (Desiree, California)

Desiree, I personally am so thankful you found the show and that you are still here helping others. You are an inspiration to me and others you have helped. Thank you for being there when I needed someone to talk to you!

> No one can help you but yourself, but if you get inspired by something, if something touches you and inspires you and makes you believe something that then helps you help yourself, then that's important.
> —Jensen Ackles

CHAPTER 5
Debbie's Story

All the people have shared very personal and fascinating stories with me, and the same goes with Debbie. She became a fan after watching the first show when it first aired. Being an old-school horror fan, she was really interested in the storyline of two brothers immersed in a world of monsters and demons. The first few episodes were a nice escape for her as she is a single mom, and watching the two brothers fight evil made for a great time. It wasn't until the fourth season, with the introduction of Castiel through his powerful entrance complete with explosions and lightning, did the show truly have her full attention. Misha Collins's portrayal of the socially awkward angel tied to the Winchester brothers was absolutely incredible. Collins's personal life before acting also resonated very deeply with Debbie as well. She too grew up in the very harsh environment of poverty and trauma, the haunting footsteps following her from childhood to adulthood.

Debbie is the youngest of six children and the only girl, so she tended to get ignored a lot and would retreat into her own world of imagination. She was the hand-me-down, thrift-shop, divorcee kid way before it was cool to shop at thrift shops. She grew up with a "challenge accepted" type attitude, and whenever life tried to beat her down, she would fight back.

Being the quirky, awkward, imaginative child in a very strict Southern Baptist household, she never felt she was truly allowed to be herself. In her opinion, watching the show was like watching her own life unfold right before her eyes at every turn. While she was in high school, she felt she was finally able to start being herself and enjoyed the freedoms that came with it. It was at this point in her life she realized she was bisexual; unfortunately, she had to hide her relationships from her mom, who was unable to understand anything that wasn't considered a normal heterosexual relationship. She doesn't blame her though; she blamed herself for being too broken to really even care.

Throughout high school and her early adult years, she says she was a lot like Dean in the fact that she embraced that "bad boy" (girl) nature, throwing herself into multiple relationships, using her body and her outgoing personality to get her through life, using friends and lovers alike as an escape from the harsh realities life had dealt her. She settled for a bad marriage at an early age, which produced two incredible children. Divorced and a single mom by the age of twenty-five, she had to pull herself and her children's lives back from the brink of poverty and homelessness time and again.

The Winchester boys went through hell multiple times for their family just as Debbie has done to save her own. She has an autistic daughter with schizophrenia and a son with a learning disability. Like Sam giving up college for his family, she has passed on several good careers for hers, choosing instead to fight for her children when no one else would. She chose to help her kids advance in life by staying home and homeschooling them, to be present in their lives and not give up on them like she feared the public school system might have. It didn't matter the sacrifice to her; her children's lives were worth it. She created her own business so they could be there alongside her during their struggles and achievements. They worked together as a team and have found many strong family members who were never blood along the way, those who stepped up when her own family failed her so many times before.

Debbie is also a GISHer. She knew of GISH for years but was never in a position to be involved till GISHMAS 2020. Joining the GISH and the bunker has become vital to her life. At the end of November 2020, it seemed Debbie's world again was falling apart as she lost her business and her home, and her second marriage of ten years broke apart. Just the week before her life fell apart, she rediscovered GISH and all the fun it brought; she always wanted to join and did so during the early registration.

Then her marriage fell apart the very next day. She went to live on her son's couch for the month of December. Christmas came and GISHmas was announced as well. The friendships she had gained online in the GISH bunker and her drive to create a new self helped to inspire her. She celebrated her forty-forth birthday on January 6 and was inspired to find her true inner self again.

She had lost sixty-eight pounds due to stress and joined GISH to get in shape and is also committed to starting a Camp GISHtopia in Alberta, Canada, where she is from. The camp is designed as a safe place for GISHers to escape to after the weeklong hunt. It has become her passion and just another way of spreading kindness and giving back to the community. She tells me that a portion of the campership will go either to a local Alberta charity or to Random Acts, the charity that is near and dear to our favorite angel's heart.

For years, Debbie has been outspoken herself about embracing your failures and fighting to reclaim your life with the mantra "challenge accepted" and to live by the motto You are never too old to learn and never too young to make a difference. Inspire others through just being your best self. You never know who is watching or how one small act can make the difference in someone's life. Those who struggle the most can have the most to give, and that is what is also the biggest take away from *Supernatural*. The Winchesters struggled and lost many times—lost people they loved, lost themselves, and each other over fifteen years—but no matter what, they always had strength to spare and give, to help, to save those who couldn't save themselves.

I so loved talking to Debbie and her "challenge accepted" attitude! She is such an inspiration, and as a GISHer myself, I do really hope she sees her dream of Camp GISHtopia to its fulfillment—that would be such an awesome place to go to, just to hang out and chill with other GISHers. Good luck to you, Debbie! Stay weird and wonderful!

> One of the things that I like to do in life is attacking things that seem impossible, and then accomplishing them, and sort of shattering the boundaries of what we think is possible. That's one of the things that I get excited about.
> —Misha Collins

CHAPTER 6

Lisa's Story

Lisa is one of my international interviewees; she lives all the way in Germany. Really the only hurdle we had was finding the right time to communicate back and forth with each other. Since the interview, we have kept in touch with each other via Facebook.

Supernatural first aired on German television in 2007, and that's when Lisa first watched and became a fan. She says she relates the most to Dean because of his loyalty and the love he feels for his family and friends, but she also feels the same weight of responsibility that goes along with that. Dean carries the weight of the world on his shoulders for the ones he cares about and believes that their safety is his sole responsibility—and Lisa can really relate to those feelings.

Some of the things she really loves about the show is how through seasons 1 through 5, for example, how the story arched and the characters grew and matured over those first five seasons, keeping her on her toes.

She also loves how easily at times the show was able to transition from seriousness into some type of comic relief or even at times have an episode that was a little on the lighter side, such as episodes like "Mystery Spot" (S3 E11), "Changing Channels" (S5 E8), and "The French Mistake" (S6 E15) and how the writers not only used the fourth wall but basically smashed it down, especially in "The French Mistake." Lisa also enjoys how the writers were always playing with and inserting different types of pop-culture references throughout the show, whether it was the boys' fake FBI names to the classic rock songs, even using references to the actors' past roles in different shows.

Many fans have come out since the final episode. Some were disappointed on how it ended, some were happy, but no matter how they feel about the actual last show, one thing is certain: we are all glad we actually got a last show. Lisa is no exception. She says that unlike many shows that never get to see a final episode, *Supernatural* fans got that chance, especially with everything that was happening in the world at the time. She also loved the final episode and thought it was a perfect ending for the show. It was heartbreaking and beautiful all at the same time, and the only thing that she would have changed was that Castiel would have been able to be in the final episode with the boys as well. Castiel died before the Winchesters and was not in the final episode at all.

The impact that *Supernatural* has had on her in life isn't so much the show itself but the actors themselves and what they have done behind the scenes such as AKF and GISH. Lisa was introduced to GISH (then still GISHWHES) in 2015 and is still active with it today. She is now a team captain of an international team. SHOUT-OUT TO THE MAD HATTERS! And GISH has had an enormous impact on her life. She has never met a community that is more kind, open-minded, and creative than the GISH community.

She loves the fact that she has found a bunch of equally weird people who are also kind. In a world like ours where politicians often are loud and hateful, it is like a breath of fresh air to know that there are other voices in this world. We might be quieter, but she will be eternally grateful to Misha Collins for showing every single one of us that we do have a voice and that we can have an impact simply by being kind, by being creative, or by being supportive. To Lisa, this knowledge makes a difference also in her personal life because she finally feels that she has found a group of humans with beliefs similar to hers—something that gives her hope for mankind and shows her that she is not alone.

On a more personal and less political level, GISH has taught her to embrace her creativity that was buried under all her adult responsibilities for a long time. Every time she plays GISH, she pushes her personal boundaries a little further, and each time she grows because of it. Lisa says it is so liberating to not care any longer what a random stranger on the street thinks about her. In fact, the more she embraces her inner weirdness, the stronger it gets, and it is an awesome feeling.

Her message to all the cast members is this:

> Thank you for bringing this awesome story and characters to life for us viewers and fans. Thank you for taking us on a journey where we laughed and cried with you and through you, where we were kept on the edge of our seats about your character's fate and where we were always rooting for the good and the love. And last but not least, thank you for showing a world in which family and love are more important than anything else. We need more of this.

Lisa also has a message for Misha Collins as well:

> Thank you for giving me the chance to dance in an inflatable bumblebee costume in a public zoo or for getting a pedicure in the middle of a concert crowd right in front of the stage. Thank you for bringing out my inner child and creativity again. And thank you for being a beacon of light and hope in times where hate and greed are usually so much louder than kindness and love. (Lisa, Germany)

She will be eternally grateful for you.

> Don't pressure yourself. Don't worry about what others think you should do or what the societal "norm" is. Do what moves you and makes you smile, and the "good" will follow.
> —Misha Collins

CHAPTER 7

Victoria's Story

Victoria is another international fan whom I met, hailing all the way from the UK. She was also the very first person to respond to my interview request. I only remember this because my phone went off in the middle of the night due to our time difference. I also remember apologizing a lot to her and getting off-topic because I was very nervous; I hadn't thought I would get one response, let alone one all the way from Europe.

Victoria, like me, hasn't been a die-hard fan as long as others have, as she wasn't introduced to the show until 2018. She recalls that it was wintertime and she and her now ex-partner were broke, so they borrowed some DVDs to watch that just happened to be, you guessed it, *Supernatural.* After the first episode, she was hooked (I seem to be seeing a pattern here), and she began binge-watching a couple of the seasons, finally getting caught up and finishing out the series in 2020.

From there she joined a Facebook fan group page so she could connect with other fans of the show, and that is where she found a mental health group filled with fans and fueled with positive messages from Jensen and Jared. While being in that group, she met someone who would later become a good friend, through whom she was invited to join GISH and be on their team during the Halloween Hunt of 2020. She treasures the friendship that came from the chance meeting in the Facebook group and hopes that someday they will be able to meet face to face and do strange GISH stuff together while

Supernatural is on the TV in the background. I personally think that would be so very cool myself.

Victoria says it was about this time she began dating someone new. She says he is very nice and quiet...sometimes too quiet. They decided to take a weekend holiday together that happened to be the same weekend as the GISH hunt, and she explained it all to him, what it was about, what it all may entail, and about the charity and good works that come from. To her surprise, he really was interested in it—a reaction she had not expected. She says they had the best weekend of their life, fangirling with him and all her online friends trying to watch Misha, who is always the master of ceremonies for the hunts on Zoom, and not being able to get it to work properly. I told her I had the same problems with mine when I was trying Zoom also for that particular hunt. She really wanted to let Misha know how much fun they had making incredibly messy pumpkin volcanos in a very small hotel room and to also let him know that she loves him very much.

She wants to give a big shout-out to the entire GISH community. She says she has never met a more diverse, weird, random, wonderful, and—most importantly—kind group of people all rolled into one, all in one place before. She just simply wants to say thank you to Misha, Jensen, Jared, and everyone involved. Thank you for all you do.

Victoria, I couldn't have said it better myself about the GISH community. You don't have to be the next Picasso or anything like that. Just have an open mind and be willing to have fun and let your creativity out! I have found that they are always there supporting one another too.

> Perhaps I shifted from "me" to "we"
> when I realized that "I" could get
> a lot more done with "us."
> —Misha Collins

CHAPTER 8

Cole's Story

Cole is thirty years old and hails from the sunshine state of Florida. Some may call him a "super fan" due to his extensive *Supernatural* memorabilia collection, which I had an opportunity to see via pictures. He is especially proud of his Funko Pop collection. He has both Dean with Baby and Sam with Baby, along with other characters from the show. He was also very proud to show me his #AKF tattoo that is on his lower arm; he says it's a reminder to him of not only how much the show and the campaign both mean to him but a daily reminder to always keep fighting.

Cole suffers from major depression and general anxiety disorders along with OCD. He also suffers from avascular necrosis and is in need of a double hip replacement. He had to stop during our interview because of a specific OCD routine he does daily and felt bad for it, at which point, I let him know it was not a problem and that I totally understood. Cole has dealt with suicidal ideations in the past but thankfully has never followed through on those thoughts. However, he has done self-harm to himself in the form of cutting.

Cole became a fan in much the same way as everyone else. He watched the first episode, and he was hooked. He claims one of the two characters he relates the most to are either Dean, because they both like to bury their feelings away and possibly drink too much, or Charlie, because he is a total nerd. Don't feel bad, Cole, so am I.

One of his favorite episodes is the crossover episode "Scooby Natural" (S13 E6), where the boys get sucked into Dean's favorite cartoon Scooby-Doo. Scoob and the gang team up with the Winchesters and Castiel to solve a real mystery. He is also a fan of "Lazarus Rising" (S4 E1). It is the first appearance of Misha Collins as Castiel the angel, as well as the episodes that followed where Castiel really didn't have a grasp or understanding of humans and their way of doing things. For instance, there is a scene where the boys are researching and not paying attention to what their angelic friend is watching on TV when Castiel says, "If the pizza man truly loves the babysitter, why does he keep slapping her rear?" at which point the boys realize he is watching.

Cole has very mixed feelings on the series finale. He says he likes the fact that it ended with the brothers being reunited at the end. However, he wasn't a big fan of how Dean died. He would have liked to see more of past cast members in the finale, though due do COVID restrictions, he understood why it was done the way it was.

Cole says that *Supernatural* has changed his life completely. He has what he calls his *Supernatural* parents, who also live in Florida and whom he FaceTimes every day and he loves dearly. He has made so many new friends through the different Facebook groups, and we both made a new friend in each other through this interview. We now message each other on a fairly regular basis just to check in on each other.

Cole plans on attending an upcoming convention in Orlando that he has been saving for, which has been pushed back twice already due to the pandemic. He is really looking forward to it. Cole is also the only one I have interviewed who has met a member of the cast; he met Felicia Day (Charlie) via an online convention. Cole is also a big fan of Radio Company and owns the first album on vinyl. He participated in a GISH hunt once and was a little unsure of how he felt about it but says he will definitely give it another shot.

Cole's message to the cast is simply thank you. "You have all changed my life, and it will never be the same. And to Jared, because of AKF, I am still alive, thank you. Love you all. Always Keep Fighting" (Cole, Florida).

> There's no shame in having to fight every
> day. *If you're still alive* to hear these words
> or read this interview, *then you are winning
> your war*. You're here. (Emphasis added)
> —Jared Padalecki

CHAPTER 9

Jennifer H.'s Story

Jennifer claims she was late to the *Supernatural* party, as it were, becoming a fan in 2007. She was loaned the DVD of the first season and binged it from beginning to end almost nonstop. After the first day of watching, she was hooked. She claims she doesn't have a favorite character; however, the character she loves to hate is Crowley (Mark Sheppard). She loves him in all the episodes he appears in. She jokingly says that being asked to pick one favorite character should be labeled a crime.

She says the easy answer to what her favorite or go-to episode is: "Lazarus Rising," because of the entrance of Castiel. However, when she is feeling really down, she turns to season 10 episodes 1, 2, and 3. Demon Dean and Savior Sam pull her right out of any funk she is in. "Yellow Fever" (S4 E6), with the outtake at the end of Jensen Ackles lip-syncing to "Eye of the Tiger," along with "Mystery Spot" (S3 E11), "Changing Channels" (S5 E8), and "Scooby Natural" (S13 E16) are all her top favorite episodes as well.

Jennifer says she didn't even realize that the show was having any type of impact on her at all as a person—until 2011. She had been watching Dean and Sam fight for each other, themselves, and their loved ones for years without realizing they allowed each of us as fans to channel that strength in some form or another. She admits that that may sound corny to some people; however, it is true. Jennifer credits the show and the strength and determination of the characters in helping her find her own strength to end an extremely abusive relationship before it became the end of her. The relationship had left her scarred, and PTSD ruled her life. Then Jared came out with his own story and started AKF and again she found the strength to stop the self-mutilation and ask for help. Both Jensen and Misha also had a hand in helping find her strength as well. Jensen used to be very shy when it came to his singing ability and was able to overcome it, and it showed Jennifer that even our heroes and idols have fears that they have to overcome in life.

Misha helped through GISH, where Jennifer was allowed to just be herself and embrace her own weirdness and uniqueness and not be judged or bullied for it, which, in turn, has led her down a path of being able to be more open with her own talents. The show and the actors showed her a way to self-happiness by showing the fans that it is possible to fight your own inner demons and win. Jennifer doesn't believe that when the show started the writers had no idea what they were creating and the lasting impact they would have by writing the incredible stories they did, nor did the actors know what kind of personal impact they were making on the fans in the beginning, though she is certainly glad they did, and she is proud to call herself part of the family.

Jennifer is also a collector of memorabilia from the show. She says she has everything from books to posters to plushies, socks, and charms, and the list goes on. Most of what she gets she orders through Stands; it is a charity-based organization for different actors and actresses to sell merchandise, and the proceeds go to their favorite charity. Many in the *Supernatural* cast use Stands, such as Jared Padalecki, Misha Collins, Jake Able, Rob Benedict, Samantha Smith, Kim Rhodes, and Alex Calvert, to name a few. CultureFly is another place that Jennifer gets her merchandise from. She has a subscription to them to receive *Supernatural* "mystery boxes," all authentic merchandise, yet the buyer has no idea what is coming. She actually talked me into purchasing one of the boxes as I can be easily persuaded, and I checked them out.

Just like everyone else, Jennifer also has mixed feelings about the final episode. She wishes they would have brought Castiel back for the final show, but overall she believes they all did the best they could, given the circumstances at the time, having to completely rewrite the last episode to fit the pandemic rules and regulations for social distancing. Like many of us, Jennifer says the final episode absolutely destroyed her; she cried off and on for three weeks. I can definitely sympathize; I cried myself to sleep that night.

Jennifer's message is to the entire cast: "Thank you! Thank you for caring and sharing your own personal battles and triumphs and giving us hope" (Jennifer).

> Always keep fighting. I'm serious. You
> know, even if you think you're alone, even
> if you think that there's no one else to listen
> to you. I disagree. You're not alone."
> —Jensen Ackles

CHAPTER 10

Gardenia's Story

Gardenia, I believe, is one of the youngest fans I have interviewed as she was eleven years old when she started watching the show. She recalls seeing the trailers for it and being excited to watch even before it ever aired. She says she was glued to her seat that entire first episode and every episode after. Gardenia's all-time, number 1 favorite episode is "Woman in White," otherwise known as the pilot (S1 E1). Not because it's the very first show but because of where Gardenia herself comes from.

Originally from Guadalajara, the story of the "Woman in White" is very culturally relevant to her and reminded her of stories she would hear as a little girl in Mexico, which is another part of the draw of the show. Eric Kripke himself admitted to being fascinated with urban legends when he was younger. A lot of the first season's episodes deal with just that subject—different variations of the scary stories we probably have all heard around a campfire or at a slumber party. Along with the pilot episode, Gardenia says one of her other favorite episodes is "Wishful Thinking" (S4 E8). In her opinion, not only was it cleverly written, but it has a very good message attached to it: be careful what you wish for.

Gardenia has been following GISH since 2018 and participated in her first mini-hunt during the Halloween hunt in 2020. She is also involved in two separate GISH writing groups and a GISH Spanish group. One of the writing groups is where she and I met. Gardenia says that both *Supernatural* and GISH have allowed her to feel like she is free to be who she wants to be and enjoy what she wants to enjoy. Together, they have brought so many people together in such a beautiful and unimaginable way. And this has left a permanent mark on her heart.

Gardenia's message is this: "Thank you for always being there. For the laughter, the tears. For helping me to realize who I am and what I am capable of accomplishing. For bringing me closer to my family and letting me be a part of a new one. What you (the cast) have achieved cannot be surpassed, nor can it be broken" (Gardenia, California).

CHAPTER 11

Jennifer T.'s Story

Your heroes wear capes
Ours wear flannel, plaid shirts.

Jennifer's first experience with *Supernatural* began in 2006, when her son came to her and told her about the show and how much she would like it. She found that her son was right on the money and almost immediately she was (say it with me) hooked. Jennifer says in all reality she has too many favorite characters to pick just one, but if she honestly had to choose, she would say that it would be a toss-up between Dean and Sam. She loves Dean's manly side and Sam's sensitive side.

While Jennifer loves all fifteen seasons, the one that stands out the most is the first episode of season 4 and Castiel's entrance with all the sparks and special effects that went along with it. The look on Dean's face when he realized he couldn't kill Castiel—because he wasn't a monster or a demon and that, in fact, he was the one who pulled him out of hell—was priceless. Castiel, on the other hand, while having this awesome entrance and being shot and stabbed by Dean, still remained to have almost a childlike, innocent look on his face while talking to Dean, trying to figure him out; Jennifer was in awe of his expressions.

Jennifer considers herself a "super fan," or as her kids like to say, she's obsessed. Don't feel bad; I hear the same from my own kids. She claims to have so much memorabilia that it's unreal—everything from blankets to jewelry to posters and clothing. Jennifer says it was a running joke in her house that either Sam or Dean was going to be her kids' new stepdad. Honestly, I am sure my kids would have been okay with that.

In all seriousness, though, Jennifer does have some amazing kids as they have come together and purchased their mom a gold package for the next *Supernatural* convention coming to Charlotte. Those packages are not cheap by any means, but it offers the fan a three-day unforgettable experience to be up close and personal with the cast. And Jennifer says she's going, come hell or high water.

According to Jennifer, the show has actually brought her own family closer together as her father was the one who introduced her son to the show first, and eventually it became family night to sit and watch the show all together. When they watched the series finale as a family, Jennifer says she cried like a baby. Her sixteen-year-old daughter gave her a funny look and was like, "Mom, it's just a TV show." Jennifer says it was much more than that; she felt it deeply. She has never watched a show before where she felt so in tune with the characters and could feel what they felt, nor has she ever seen such an outpouring of support among the fans for one another on social media after the show ended. It was absolutely amazing.

Jennifer has a message she would like to give to Jared: "I think that he is an amazing person inside and out. I love the AKF message, and it has helped me immensely with my own battles with depression. I also hope when I go to the convention, I'll get the chance to tell them all what they mean to me" (Jennifer T. Charlotte).

You're stronger than you think! Just keep fighting
and keep your head up. You need to smile more;
it's too pretty for you to hide it all the time.
                                        —Jared Padalecki

THE ROAD CONTINUES

So here we all stand at the end of one road—the cast, crew and fans alike. So what next? We keep going, keep fighting and writing our own stories. We will all go down our paths and roads now knowing that no matter where we go, we are never far from family—those who have our backs, no matter how bad it gets.

These stories are just the tip of the iceberg. There are so many more to tell, many more lives changed for the better, many more bonds made. Awareness has been made about a number of silent and not-so-silent issues, not just in our country but around the world, and solutions are being found not by politicians but by everyday people through creativity and out-of-the-box thinking.

I have finally come around full circle in my life. I am no longer ashamed of my past or who I once was. I am able to go back to seeing the glass as half-full again and embrace both the good and bad days that come because there is always someone there when I reach out, and I have been able to be the hand that reaches back for someone else when they need it. I also recently applied for the IMAlive online crisis team to become a volunteer crisis counselor. I am of the opinion that a lot of the organizations and the people who have been helped by them would not either exist or have had the impact they have had, had it not been for *Supernatural* and its success. It was a little show with a huge impact. The seed was planted in 2005 and from it grew a family tree with millions of branches, and it's okay if people don't get it, but to the ones who do, we have found hope where there was once none. On the surface, the show is horror/sci-fi, and it's storytelling at its finest—the hero's journey, as it were—and touches us all emotionally to the point that even though they are fictional, we feel their pain because we have felt it on some level.

So carry on, wayward sons and daughters. The road will and does continue, just in new directions.

You are never alone.

My bones can be
Scorched from fires
Broken by
Betrayals
Stained with
Blood
And I will keep fighting

ABOUT THE AUTHOR

Kellie is an advocate for not only mental health and suicide prevention but also for epilepsy awareness and disabled veterans.

In her spare time, she enjoys the outdoors as much as possible and spending time with her family.

Her greatest inspiration for this book was just living life and knowing the ups and downs and trials and tribulations everyone faces, regardless of status in life. Her hope is this that these stories touch you the same way they touched her and that they inspire and help someone.

9 781638 815891